Norman Rockwell's

George Mendoza

Americana A B C

Dell Publishing Co., Inc.

Harry N. Abrams, Inc., Publishers, New York

For *Paul Anbinder,* man of patience, child of spirit . . .

With special thanks to *Ted Maass*

Library of Congress Cataloging in Publication Data

Rockwell, Norman, 1894–
    Norman Rockwell's Americana A B C.

    SUMMARY: The letters of the alphabet are
introduced through paintings and poetry on an
American theme.
    1. Rockwell, Norman, 1894–   –Juvenile
literature. 2. United States in art–Juvenile
literature. 3. Alphabet–Juvenile literature.
4. Mendoza, George–Illustrations–Juvenile literature. [1. Alphabet books. 2. Rockwell, Norman,
1894–   3. United States in art] I. Mendoza,
George. II. Title. III. Title: Americana A B C.
ND237.R68M46 1975   759.13   75-8886
ISBN 0-440-05944-5
ISBN 0-440-05939-9 lim. ed., signed

Library of Congress Catalogue Card Number: 75-8886
Copyright ©1975 by Harry N. Abrams, Incorporated, New York
The illustrations that accompany the following letters of the alphabet
in this book are copyrighted © by:
Curtis Publishing Company: C and D, 1923; H, 1927; U and W, 1928; E, 1934.
J, 1939; V, 1947; O, 1948; P, 1951; Z, 1952; M, 1954; X, 1958; F, 1959;
G, 1961
Norman Rockwell for *Look* magazine: A and N, 1967
Brown & Bigelow, Minnesota: S, 1948
Printed and bound in the United States of America

The lines from the song *Zip-A-Dee Doo Dah* are used by permission of
the Robbins Music Corporation, New York

Who am I?
I am America
as deep and warm,
great and tall,
as Norman Rockwell painted me…

norman rockwell

I am an astronaut
on my way to the stars…

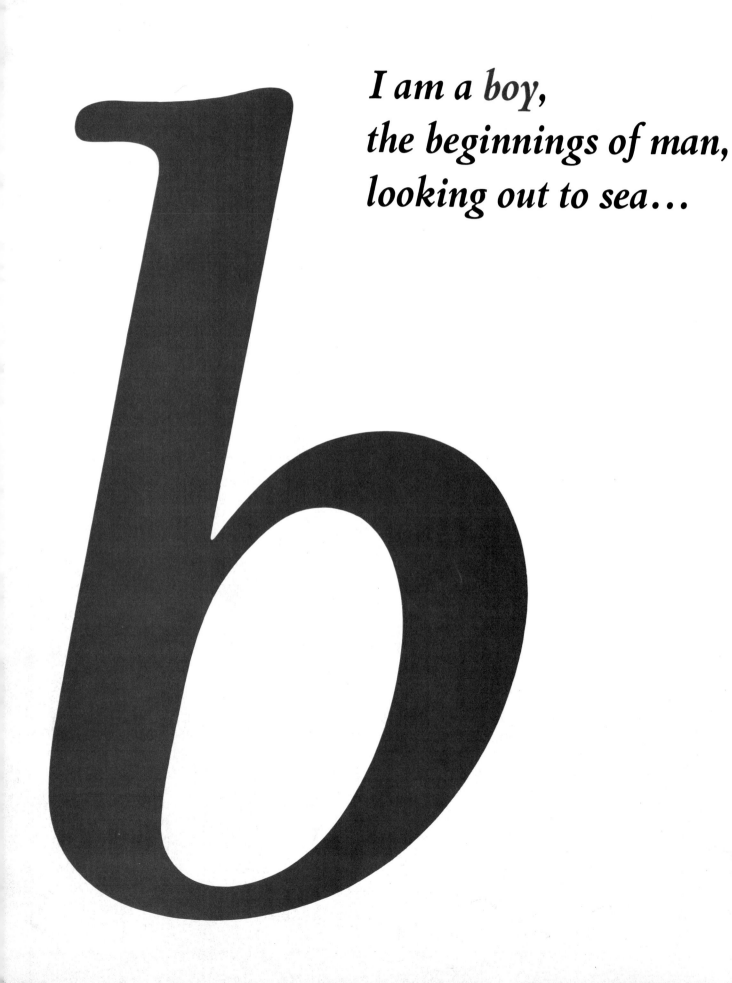

I am a boy,
the beginnings of man,
looking out to sea…

I am Christmas and carols
that I wish would stay all year...

I am a dancer
tapping out dreams...

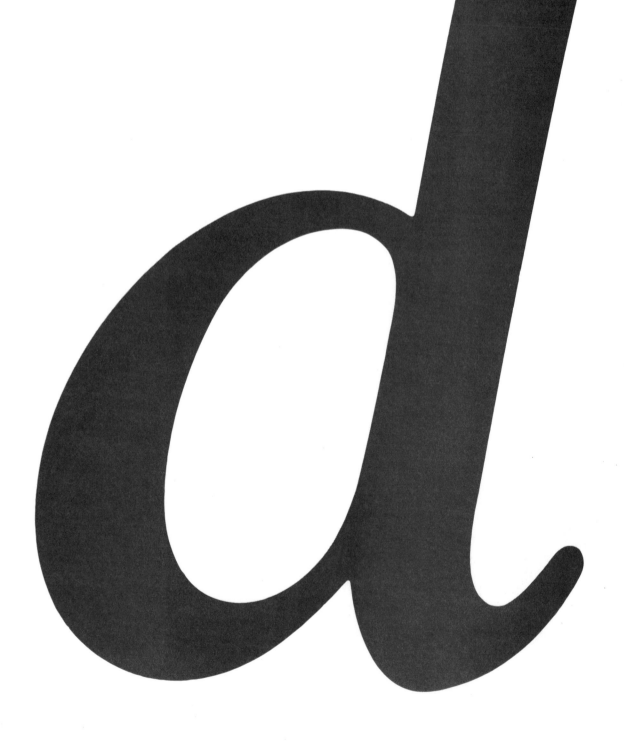

I am the end of the rainbow
where you will find
the land of enchantment…

f

I am a *family* tree.
Do you know where
you came from…?

a Family Tree by norman rockwell

I am the Golden *Rule,*
a good *idea to think about…*

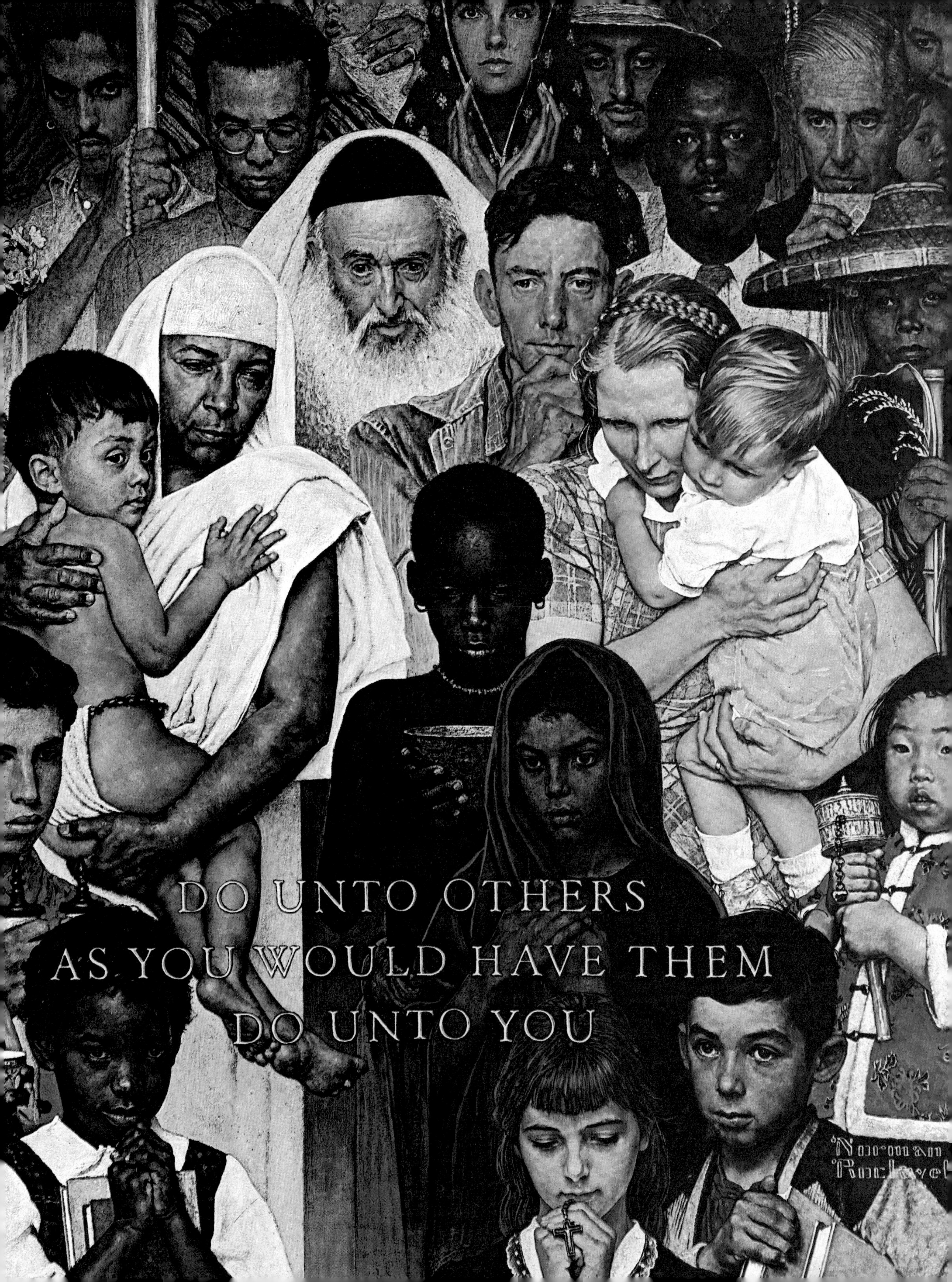

DO UNTO OTHERS
AS YOU WOULD HAVE THEM
DO UNTO YOU

*I am a heart of love
that means
you're mine forever...*

I am an ice-skater
with a young boy's way...

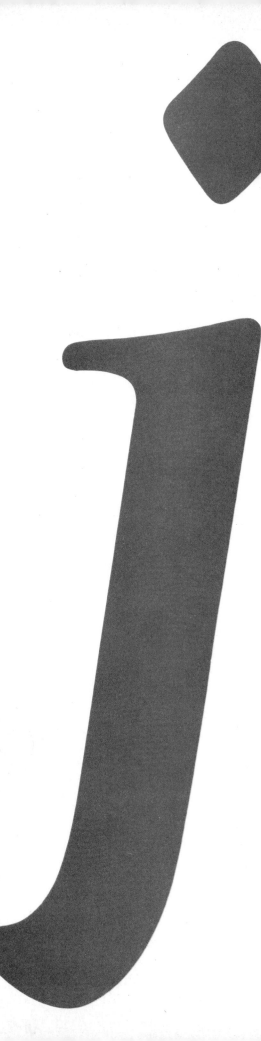

*I am a jester,
a clown
sometimes happy
and sometimes sad…*

*I am a **kite**-flyer*
fishing for clouds…

I am the land as far as I can see,
before and after me…

NORMAN ROCKWELL

*I am a mirror filled with
the magic of tomorrow…*

I am your new neighbor
and soon we will play together…

I am old MacDonald
who had a farm,
E-I-E-I-O...

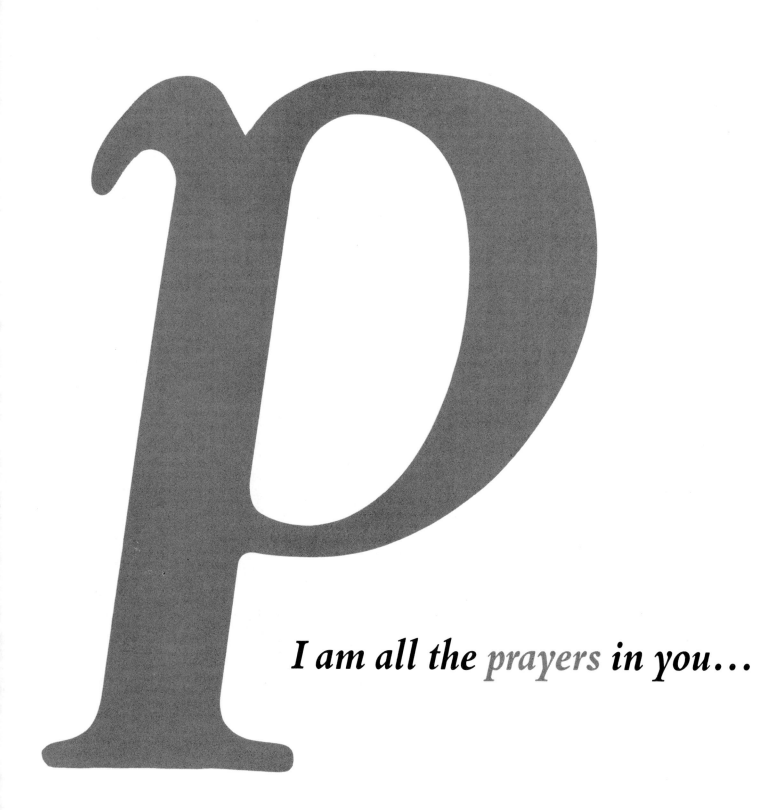

I am all the prayers in you…

I am the quiet time of each falling night…

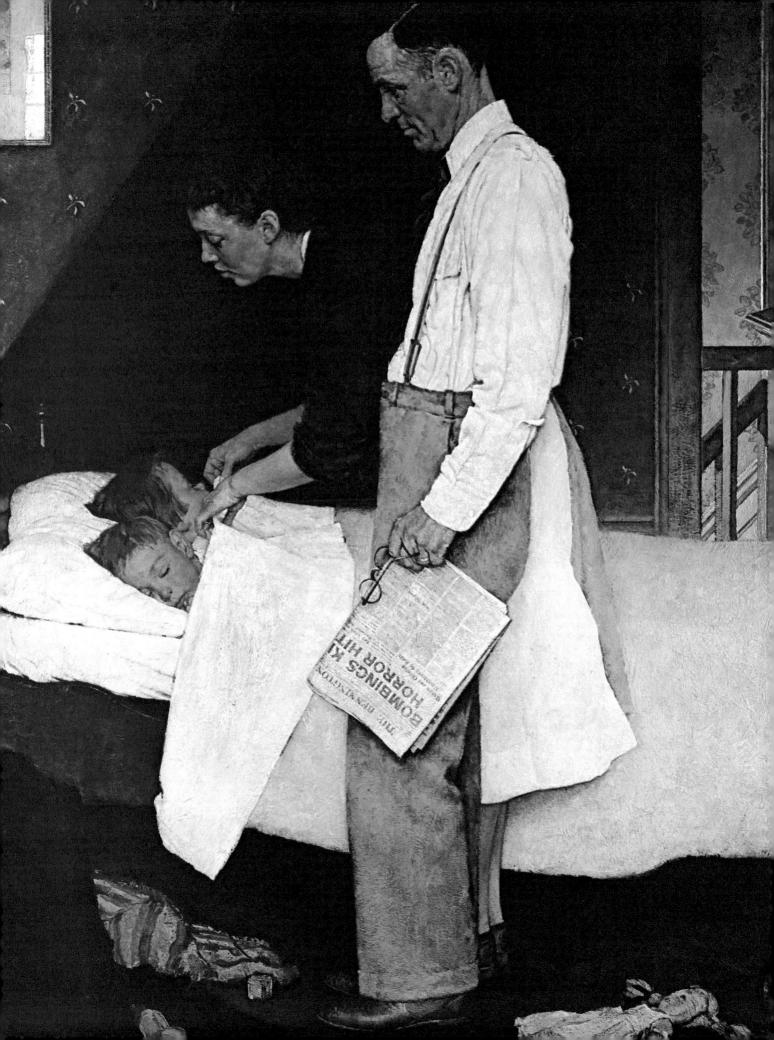

*I am a riverboat race
up the Connecticut
coming hard…*

I am the seasons of the year,
a revolving door
for all the things you like to do...

Norman
Rockwell

*I am the turkey on your table
and the joy of giving thanks…*

I am Uncle Sam
and I am going to fly
with you forever…

To my
good friend
Bob Savage

Norman
Rockwell

*I am vacation time,
eager for it,
O glad it's over…*

I am the wings of an eagle soaring gold...

I am the X *that marks the shot...*

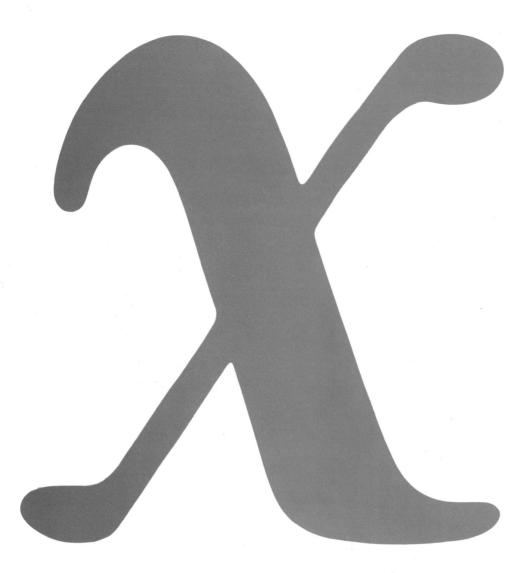

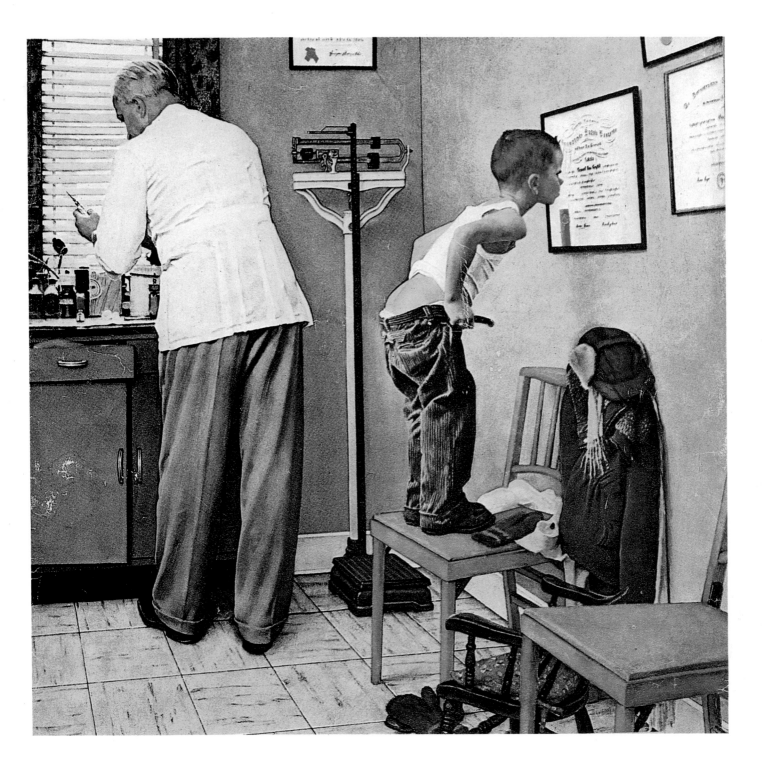

YANKEE DOODLE CAME TO TOWN · RIDING ON A PONY · STUCK A FEA

I am Yankee Doodle came to town
Riding on a pony
Stuck a feather in his hat
And called it macaroni…

IN HIS HAT · AND CALLED IT MACARONI

I am "Zip-a-dee doo-dah,
Zip-a-dee-ay,
my, oh my, what a wonderful day...

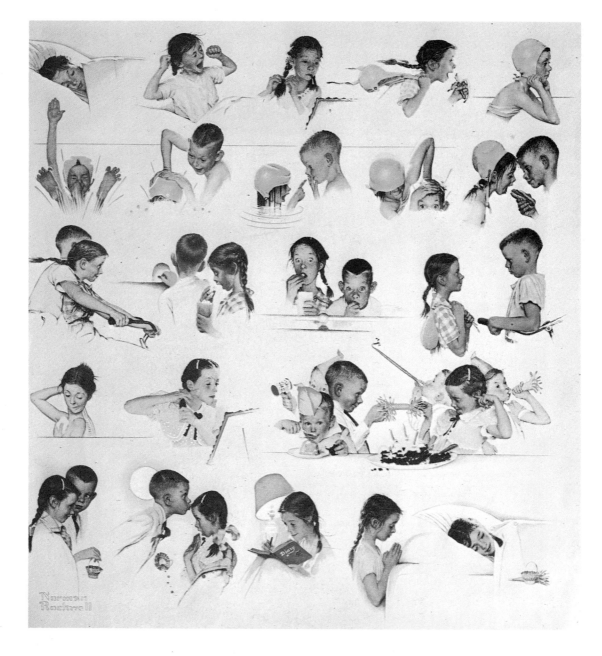

I am America.
I begin with A
and I end in a.
I am America
as long ago as I can remember
and as far ahead as I can dream.

A. *Astronauts on the Moon.* Original oil painting for *Look* illustration, January 10, 1967. Collection Aerospace Museum, Smithsonian Institution

B. *Looking out to Sea.* 1919. Original oil painting. Collection Norman Rockwell

C. *Christmas Trio.* Original oil painting for *Saturday Evening Post* cover, December 8, 1923. Collection Norman Rockwell

D. *Little Girl Dancing. Saturday Evening Post* cover, February 3, 1923

E. *The Land of Enchantment.* Original oil painting for *Saturday Evening Post* illustration, December 22, 1934. Collection New Rochelle Public Library, New York

F. *A Family Tree.* Original oil painting for *Saturday Evening Post* cover, October 24, 1959. Collection Norman Rockwell

G. *The Golden Rule.* Original oil painting for *Saturday Evening Post* cover, April 1, 1961. Collection Norman Rockwell

H. *The Young Artist.* Original oil painting for *Saturday Evening Post* cover, June 4, 1927. Collection Mr. and Mrs. William M. Young, Jr.

I. *Skater.* 1947. Original oil painting. Collection Mr. and Mrs. Howard Weingrow

J. *Jester.* Original oil painting for *Saturday Evening Post* cover, February 11, 1939. Collection Mrs. G. A. Godwin

K. *Boy Flying Kite.* 1930s drawing. Collection Dr. Robert Bakish

L. Original oil painting for the Department of the Interior, Bureau of Reclamation, 1970

M. *Girl at the Mirror.* Original oil painting for *Saturday Evening Post* cover, March 6, 1954. Berkshire Museum, on loan from Norman Rockwell

N. *New Kids in the Neighborhood.* Original oil painting for *Look* illustration, May 16, 1967

O. *A Visit to a County Agricultural Agent.* Original oil painting for *Saturday Evening Post,* July 24, 1948. Collection University of Nebraska Art Galleries, Lincoln. Gift of Nathan Gold

P. *Saying Grace.* Original oil painting for *Saturday Evening Post* cover, November 24, 1951. Collection Mr. and Mrs. Ken Stuart

Q. *Freedom from Fear.* Original oil painting for poster, 1943. Collection Norman Rockwell

R. *Steamboat Race on the Connecticut River.* Original oil painting, c. 1935. Whereabouts unknown

S. Four Seasons calendar: *Man and Boy.* Original oil paintings ©1948 by Brown and Bigelow, a Division of Standard Packaging, Saint Paul, Minnesota

T. *Freedom from Want.* Original oil painting for poster, 1943. Collection Norman Rockwell

U. *Uncle Sam.* Original oil painting for *Saturday Evening Post* cover, January 21, 1928. Collection Paul C. Wilmot

V. *A Day's Outing. Saturday Evening Post* cover, August 30, 1947

W. *Man Painting Flagpole.* Original oil painting for *Saturday Evening Post* cover, May 26, 1928. Collection the McCullough Family

X. *Before the Shot.* Original oil painting for *Saturday Evening Post* cover, March 5, 1958. Collection Dr. and Mrs. Edward F. Babbott

Y. *Yankee Doodle* mural. Nassau Tavern, Princeton, New Jersey

Z. *A Day in the Life of a Boy. Saturday Evening Post* cover, May 24, 1952, and *A Day in the Life of a Girl. Saturday Evening Post* cover, August 30, 1952.